WELLINGTON'S Way to Learn FRENCH

Penrose Colyer

Illustrated by David Lock

GRANADA

For Andrew, Angela, Bill, Catherine, Duncan and Lenka

Design: Wendi Watson
French adviser: Anne Andrault
Graphic reproduction and lettering: ReproSharp, 47 Farringdon Road, London EC1
Production: Snap Graphics Limited, 7 Newburgh Street, London W1

Published by Granada Publishing 1985
Granada Publishing Ltd
8 Grafton Street, London W1X 3LA

Colyer, Penrose
Wellington's Way to Learn French
1. French language – Juvenile literature
1. Title
448 PC2095

ISBN 0-246-12638-8

Printed and bound in Great Britain by Purnell and Sons, Bristol

Table des matières
Contents

Welliparle
Wellispeak

Wellilesson 1

This is your first lesson from me, the mighty Wellington. Pay attention!

As you read my book, you will speak French. Not necessarily out loud (people think you're funny if you do that, I don't know why, it seems quite normal to me. But then I'm not a human.) To get back to the point: you'll say French words in your head.

The question I ask myself (as it's not much good asking you, you wouldn't know) is this: will you say the words correctly? With all respect (huh!) I don't expect you will. Not unless you follow my rules.

Remember: WELLIRULES are to be OBEYED.

WELLIRULE 1: Listen to French.
"Listen to French? How can I?" I hear you asking rather crossly. "I'm not in France." True. But I expect you know someone who speaks French – your sister or brother, your parents, a friend or even a teacher. And what about all those real live French people locked up in the radio, just waiting for you to switch on and listen to them? OK, OK, I know you won't understand what they're saying. But listening to them will get you used to the different sounds the French make – some of which don't exist in English, like the French *r* which you have to roll in the back of your throat as if you were a sick bear: *rrr* . . .

When you listen, you'll notice that the French run a lot of words together, and they talk very fast. So don't try to pick out individual words – well, you can if you like, but if you get very far you're a lot cleverer than I am, and that is SAYING SOMETHING.

You'll find that if you listen to the same radio programmes a few times, some of the words will start to make sense. For example, when you've heard the French football results five or six times, you'll know the words for *nil* and *team* without a moment's hesitation (unless you're quite hopeless, which I'm not prepared to take a bet on, as you might win it).

WELLIRULE 2: Watch French people.
"Come off it!" I hear you grumbling, "You can't watch French people on radio, and my parents and brothers and sisters and friends and teachers aren't French, and none of them knows anybody French!" OK, OK. But there's television and the cinema. Not often, I admit, but often enough to be useful, you can see French people on the screen. They may be talking French which has been dubbed, so all you hear is English. That doesn't matter. (I've got an answer to all your objections, so you might as well give up making them. I am ALWAYS RIGHT.)

You'll notice (yes you will) that French people make different shapes with their mouth. They make more shapes than the British do.

When you watch French people, notice their whole face, and their hands. When they talk, it's not just their words which show their meaning. For example, when French people ask a question, their eyebrows are raised high, their hands are opened in a questioning gesture, and their heads tilt up and back a little.

WELLIRULE 3: Imitate people.
When you were a sweet little baby (ugh!) you could make only a few sounds, mostly screams and gurgles. You learned words by imitating your parents, grand-parents, brothers, sisters, and all the other people who leaned over your pram and said "How sweet!" You didn't realize that you were copying them, but you were – how else do you think you learned to talk?

Now you are old enough to realize that you can learn a lot of French by imitating. Of course the best place for doing this is France – get there if you can. But there's a lot you can do wherever you live. For example, ask your teacher or librarian or other helpful person to help you find a record or video or cassette of somebody talking French (or maybe singing). Listen carefully, pick out a few French sounds, and then practise saying (or singing) them. The results will be truly awful, and I'm glad I shan't be around to hear them. I have other things to do with my time: better, more exciting, more dangerous and SECRET things.

Back to French sounds: here are some to learn. I've told you how to say them. I've written the part of the word which you should emphasize in CAPITAL letters, for example you would say my name with the emphasis on the first part: *WELL-ing-ton.*

★ **mon** - *my.*
Try saying this little word as if it was an English word. Notice that the tip of your tongue touches the roof of your mouth (well it should). But when you pronounce it the French way, your tongue should not touch the roof of your mouth. It should stay quietly, not moving, on the floor of your mouth, because you don't pronounce the *n* at all. The *o* is nasalized, which means it's spoken as if the sound is coming from your nose rather than from your mouth (nasalized is to do with noses, like nasal spray). You can get an exaggerated version of the sound by holding your nose and practising.

★ **question** – *question.*
This is easy. In French, *qu* is spoken as if it was the *k* in English *kick*. The *n* is nasalized, which you now know about; so say *KES-ti-on.*

★ **prune** – *plum.*
This *u* sound doesn't exist in English. Say it with your lips pushed forward, in a tight little circle: *PREW-n.*

★ **frère** – *brother.*
This word contains two examples of the famous back-of-the-throat French *r*. Imagine that you're gargling. Pronounce it *FRRAIR-r.*

★ **moi** – *me.*
Another easy one. The *o* and *i* together sound like *wa*, with the *a* the same as in English *cat*. So pronounce the whole word *mwa.*

★ **couteau** - *knife.*
This sounds as if it was written *COO-toe.*

★ **soleil** – *sun* or *sunshine.*
The *o* sounds the same as in English *job*. Pronounce *eil* like the *a* in English *day*. So the whole thing is spoken *so-LAY.*

★ **deux** – *two.*
Say *er* in English. That's fairly near to the sound of *eu* in French. Say the whole thing: *der.*

★ **jeune** – *young.*
To get the sound in the middle is what you're after. It's a bit like *zh*. Say *ZHER-n.*

★ **beau** – *good-looking.*
Say *bowl* in English. Then say it without pronouncing the *l*: *bow*. Then say **Wellington est très beau** – perfect!

★ **a, e, i, o, u.**
Vowels in French have a much shorter, sharper sound than in English. For example, *a* is never spoken as it is in English *bar*. It usually sounds like the *a* in English *hat*. Sometimes it's pronounced differently – that's the trouble with human rules, they have exceptions. But WELLIRULES ARE ALWAYS RIGHT.

★ **é, è, à, â, ô, ê, î, û.**
Accents can change letters and words:
1 Accents can change the sound of a letter. For example *é* is an *e* with an acute accent, which makes a short, sharp sound (*acute* means *sharp*). For example **étoile** – *star* – is spoken *AY-twal.* The middle *e* in **frère** has a *grave* accent (**grave** is a French word, pronounced *graav*). Say *è* with your mouth open, but as if it's coming from your throat, not your mouth. Try **derrière:** say *deh-ree-AIR.*
2 Accents can change the meaning of a word. For example, *à* has an accent (*acute* or *grave?* I bet you've forgotten). The accent shows that the word *à* is different from the word *a*. For example, **patins à roulettes** are *roller skates*; but **il a un hamster** means *he's got a hamster.*
3 Accents can be just a hangover from an old-fashioned way of spelling a word. This can be useful, because the accent can help you to translate a word into English. Here's how: if you see *â, ê, î, ô* or *û,* take the accent off, and add an *s* after the letter which had the accent. So **hôpital** becomes *hospital* – the right word in English.

WELLIRULE 4: Understand short forms.
Like all languages, French has some words which are nearly always shortened. In English people don't write the word *Mister*, they write the short form *Mr.* In my book you'll find **M.**, which is the short form of **Monsieur** – *Mr/Sir,* and **Mme**, which is **Madame** – *Mrs/Madam.*

WELLIRULE 5: Obey all Wellirules.
You will get better at French, believe me (or else!).

Wellington, c'est moi!
I'm Wellington!

Je m'appelle Wellington.
I'm called Wellington.

J'habite partout dans le monde.
I live everywhere in the world.

J'ai dix ans – ou cent – ou mille – je ne sais pas!
I'm ten years old – or a hundred – or a thousand – I don't know!

Détails personnels
Personal details

Hauteur: 1.40 mètres (cou court); 1.85 mètres (cou étiré).
Height: 1.40 metres (neck short); 1.85 metres (neck extended).

Poids: Avant le petit déjeuner: 40 kilos.
Weight: Before breakfast: 40 kilos.

Après un bon repas, par exemple une calculatrice,
After a good meal, for example a calculator,

deux robinets, trois panneaux de signalisation
two taps, three road signs

et un appareil photo: 45 kilos.
and a camera: 45 kilos.

Pointure (chaussures): Déteste les chaussures, n'en porte jamais.
Size (shoes): Hate shoes, never wear any.

Signes particuliers: Cou élastique,
Special features: Elastic neck,

capacité d'être invisible aux humains
ability to be invisible to humans

et système digestif excellent.
and excellent digestive system.

Numéro de téléphone: N'en ai pas. Ai mangé le téléphone.
Telephone number: Haven't got one. Ate the telephone.

Welliquiz

Wellington est-il beau?
Is Wellington good-looking?

Oui/Non.
Yes/No.

A-t-il dix ans?
Is he ten years old?

Oui/Non/Sais pas.
Yes/No/Don't know.

Qui a mangé son téléphone?
Who ate his telephone?

Bélier
Aries
21 mars – 20 avril
March 21st – April 20th

Taureau
Taurus
21 avril – 20 mai
April 21st – May 20th

Gémeaux
Gemini
21 mai – 21 juin
May 21st – June 21st

Cancer
Cancer
22 juin – 22 juillet
June 22nd – July 22nd

Lion
Leo
23 juillet – 22 août
July 23rd – August 22nd

Vierge
Virgo
23 août – 23 septembre
August 23rd – September 23rd

Balance
Libra
24 septembre – 23 octobre
September 24th – October 23rd

Scorpion
Scorpio
24 octobre – 22 novembre
October 24th – November 22nd

Sagittaire
Sagittarius
23 novembre – 21 décembre
November 23rd – December 21st

Capricorne
Capricorn
22 décembre – 20 janvier
December 22nd – January 20th

Verseau
Aquarius
21 janvier – 18 février
January 21st – February 18th

Poissons
Pisces
19 février – 20 mars
February 19th – March 20th

Et toi?
And you?

Quand tu vois ★★, choisis les mots corrects.
When you see ★★, choose the correct words.

Wellington: Comment t'appelles-tu?
Wellington: What is your name?

Toi: Je m'appelle ★★.
You: My name is ★★.

Wellington: Quel âge as-tu?
Wellington: How old are you?

Toi: J'ai ★★ ans.
You: I'm ★★ years old.

(Exemples: (Examples:	**six** six	**sept** seven	**huit** eight
neuf nine	**dix** ten	**onze** eleven	
douze twelve	**treize** thirteen	**quatorze)** fourteen)	

Wellington: Où habites-tu?
Wellington: Where do you live?

Toi: J'habite ★★.
You: I live ★★.

(Exemples: en France, en Grande-Bretagne, aux États-Unis)
(Examples: in France, in Britain, in the United States)

Wellington: Quelle est la date de ton anniversaire?
Wellington: When is your birthday?

Toi: C'est ★★.
You: It's ★★.

(Exemples: le ler juin, le 25 avril)
(Examples: June 1st, April 25th)

Wellington: Quel est ton signe du zodiaque?
Wellington: What is your zodiac sign?

Toi: C'est ★★.
You: It's ★★.

Dans la vitrine du photographe
In the photographer's shop window

Alice et Lune.
Alice and Moon.

Ce sont des copines.
They are pals.

Jeanne Lebon et son chien Minus.
Jean Good and her dog Minus.

Henri Duval.
Henry Valley.

Il est très fort en foot.
He is very good at football.

Oncle Georges.
Uncle George.

Il a toujours l'air triste.
He always looks sad.

Yasmine est médecin.
Yasmin is a doctor.

Laure est détective.
Laura is a detective.

M. et Mme Lebon et leur fille Marie.
Mr and Mrs Good and their daughter Mary.

M. et Mme Duval et leur fils Pierre.
Mr and Mrs Valley and their son Peter.

Anne.
Anne.

Tante Delphine.
Aunt Delphine.

Welliquiz

Qu'est-ce qu'il a mordu, Wellington?
What has Wellington bitten?

Quelle est la photo la plus effrayante?
Which is the most frightening photo?

Quelle est la photo la plus amusante?
Which is the funniest photo?

David (à gauche), Jean et Guy (à droite).
David (on the left), John and Guy (on the right).

Ce sont des copains.
They are pals.

Luc.
Luke.

Il est habillé pour aller à une boum.
He is dressed to go to a party.

Isabelle.
Isobel.

Mimi et Ahmed
Mimi and Ahmed.

Ce sont des champions de patinage.
They are champion skaters.

Mémé et le bébé.
Granny and the baby.

Oncle Albert et son chat Salomon.
Uncle Albert and his cat Solomon.

Ils sont inventeurs.
They are inventors.

ELLES SONT DÉLICIEUSES, CES PHOTOS.
THESE PHOTOS ARE DELICIOUS.

Wellington aime . . .
Wellington likes . . .

Mes plats préférés
My favourite dishes

Wellington: Le chocolat, les frites et les chewing-gums ne m'intéressent pas.
Wellington: Chocolates, chips and chewing gum don't interest me.

J'aime manger les objets faits en métal, en bois et en plastique.
I like eating things made of metal, wood and plastic.

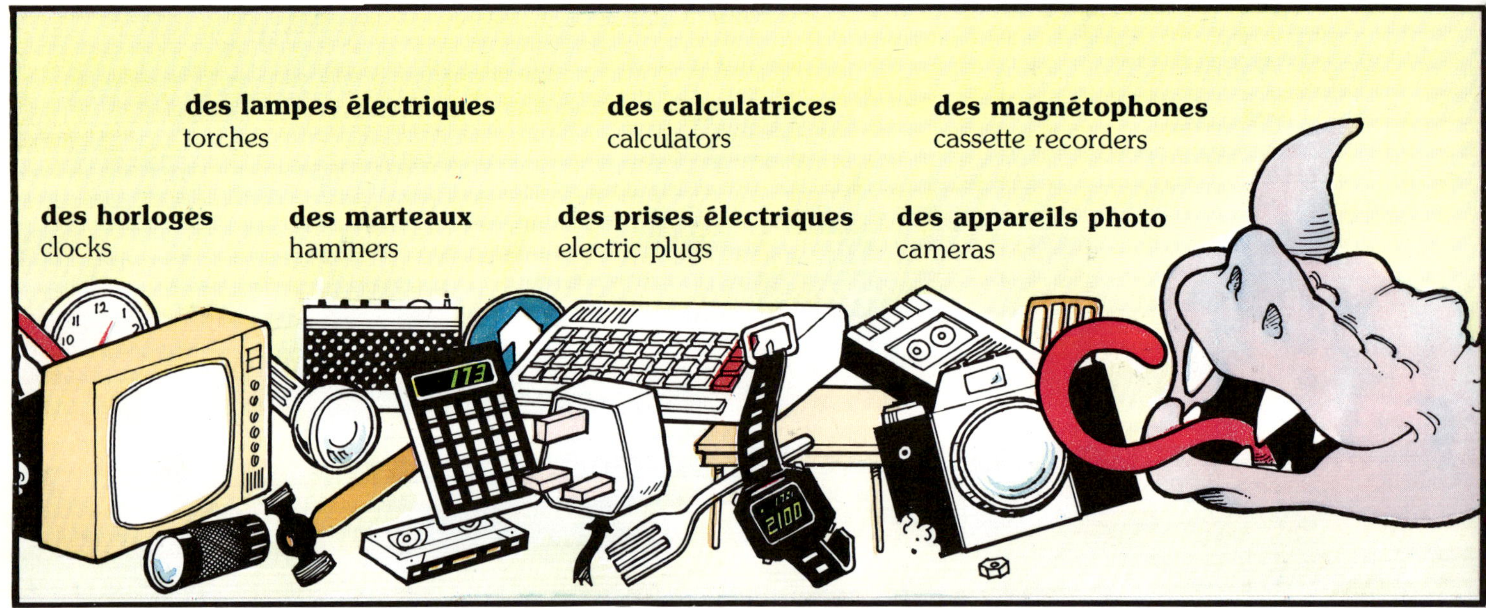

Quand les objets sont trop gros à avaler, je mords dedans.
When things are too big to swallow, I take a bite out of them.

Par exemple: les ordinateurs, les téléviseurs et les chaises.
For example: computers, television sets and chairs.

Mes activités préférées
My favourite activities

En premier: Manger et mordre des objets.
First: Eating and biting things.

Ensuite: Embrouiller les humains.
Next: Confusing humans.

Mais quelquefois je les aide.
But sometimes I help them.

Mes copains
My pals

Minus: J'aime Wellington, mais quelquefois j'ai peur de lui.
Minus: I like Wellington, but sometimes I'm afraid of him.

Henri Duval: J'aime bien Wellington.
Henry Valley: I like Wellington.

Mais il mange toujours mes calculatrices.
But he always eats my calculators.

Je déteste ça.
I hate that.

Tante Delphine: Je suis une très grande fan de Wellington. C'est mon héros.
Aunt Delphine: I'm a great fan of Wellington. He's my hero.

Welliquiz

Quels sont tes plats préférés? Les hamburgers? Les glaces?
What are your favourite dishes? Hamburgers? Ice-creams?

Quelles sont tes activités préférées? Le sport? La musique? Les jeux électroniques?
What are your favourite activities? Sports? Music? Computer games?

Comment s'appellent tes meilleurs copains et copines?
What are the names of your best friends?

Comment s'appellent tes héros et tes héroïnes?
What are the names of your heroes and heroines?

Comment s'appellent tes parents? Tes frères et sœurs?
What are the names of your parents? Your brothers and sisters?

Tes tantes et oncles? Tes grands-parents?
Your aunts and uncles? Your grand-parents?

Les couleurs de l'arc-en-ciel
The colours of the rainbow

Voici un arc-en-ciel composé de fruits.
Here is a rainbow made up of fruit.

Il y a des fraises, des prunes, des oranges, du raisin,
There are strawberries, plums, oranges, grapes,

des pommes et des bananes.
apples and bananas.

De quelle couleur sont les fruits?
What colour are the fruits?

Complète ces phrases.
Complete these sentences.

Les ★★ sont rouges.
The ★★ are red.

Les ★★ sont bleues.
The ★★ are blue.

Les ★★ sont orange.
The ★★ are orange.

Le ★★ est violet.
The ★★ are violet.

Les ★★ sont vertes.
The ★★ are green.

Les ★★ sont jaunes.
The ★★ are yellow.

Un sweatshirt blanc.
A white sweatshirt.

Une robe marron.
A brown dress.

Un pantalon bleu foncé.
Dark blue trousers.

Vrai ou faux: Lune a les cheveux blonds?
True or false: Moon has got blonde hair?

Comment s'appelle ce garçon?
What is this boy called?

Une chemise bleu clair.
A pale blue shirt.

Une chemise grise.
A grey shirt.

Une jupe rose.
A pink skirt.

Un short noir.
Black shorts.

Vrai ou faux: Cette jeune fille aime les couleurs claires?
True or false: This girl likes pale colours?

Le mariage de Marie et de Pierre
Mary and Peter's wedding

Voici la photo de mariage de Marie Lebon et Pierre Duval.
Here is the wedding photo of Mary Good and Peter Valley.

Laure est la tante de Marie.
Laura is Mary's aunt.

Le perroquet s'appelle Plume.
The parrot is called Feather.

Il s'est échappé du zoo.
It escaped from the zoo.

Georges est l'oncle de Pierre.
George is Peter's uncle.

Il est champion de billard.
He is a snooker champion.

Henri est le neveu de Pierre.
Henry is Peter's nephew.

Il n'aime pas les mariages.
He does not like weddings.

Il aime les ordinateurs et les souris.
He likes computers and mice.

Le père et la mère de Marie.
Mary's father and mother.

Comment s'appellent-ils?
What are they called?

Marie aime Pierre.
Mary loves Peter.

Elle est heureuse.
She is happy.

Pierre aime Marie.
Peter loves Mary.

Il est heureux.
He is happy.

La mère de Pierre s'appelle Madame Duval.
Peter's mother is called Mrs Valley.

Elle a chaud.
She is hot.

Le père de Pierre aide sa femme.
Peter's father is helping his wife.

Welliquiz

Combien de souris vois-tu?
How many mice can you see?

Où est la bague de Marie?
Where is Mary's ring?

Alice est la nièce de Marie.
Alice is Mary's niece.

Elle veut être adulte.
She wants to be a grown-up.

Elle aime le maquillage.
She likes make-up.

La sœur de Marie s'appelle Jeanne.
Mary's sister is called Jean.

Elle pleure.
She is crying.

Mais elle est heureuse.
But she is happy.

Son chien Minus l'adore.
Her dog Minus adores her.

Wellington chez lui
Wellington at home

Wellington ne mord ni ne mange ses propres objets.
Wellington does not bite or eat his own things.

Mais la semaine dernière, il avait tellement faim qu'il a mangé son propre téléphone.
But last week he was so hungry that he ate his own telephone.

Donc un ingénieur des téléphones lui apporte un téléphone neuf.
So a telephone engineer is bringing him a new telephone.

Wellington a oublié de se faire invisible aux humains.
Wellington has forgotten to make himself invisible to humans.

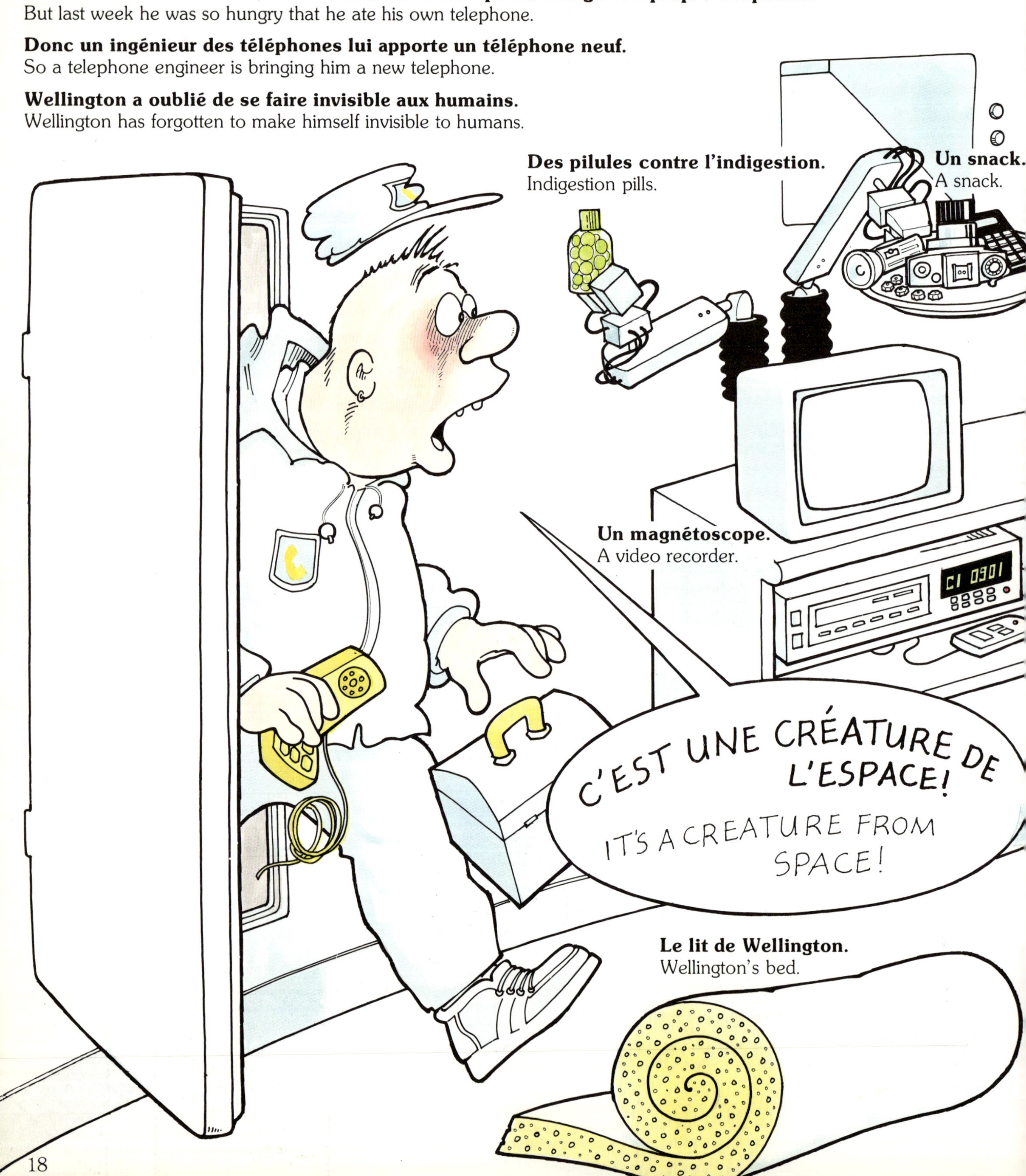

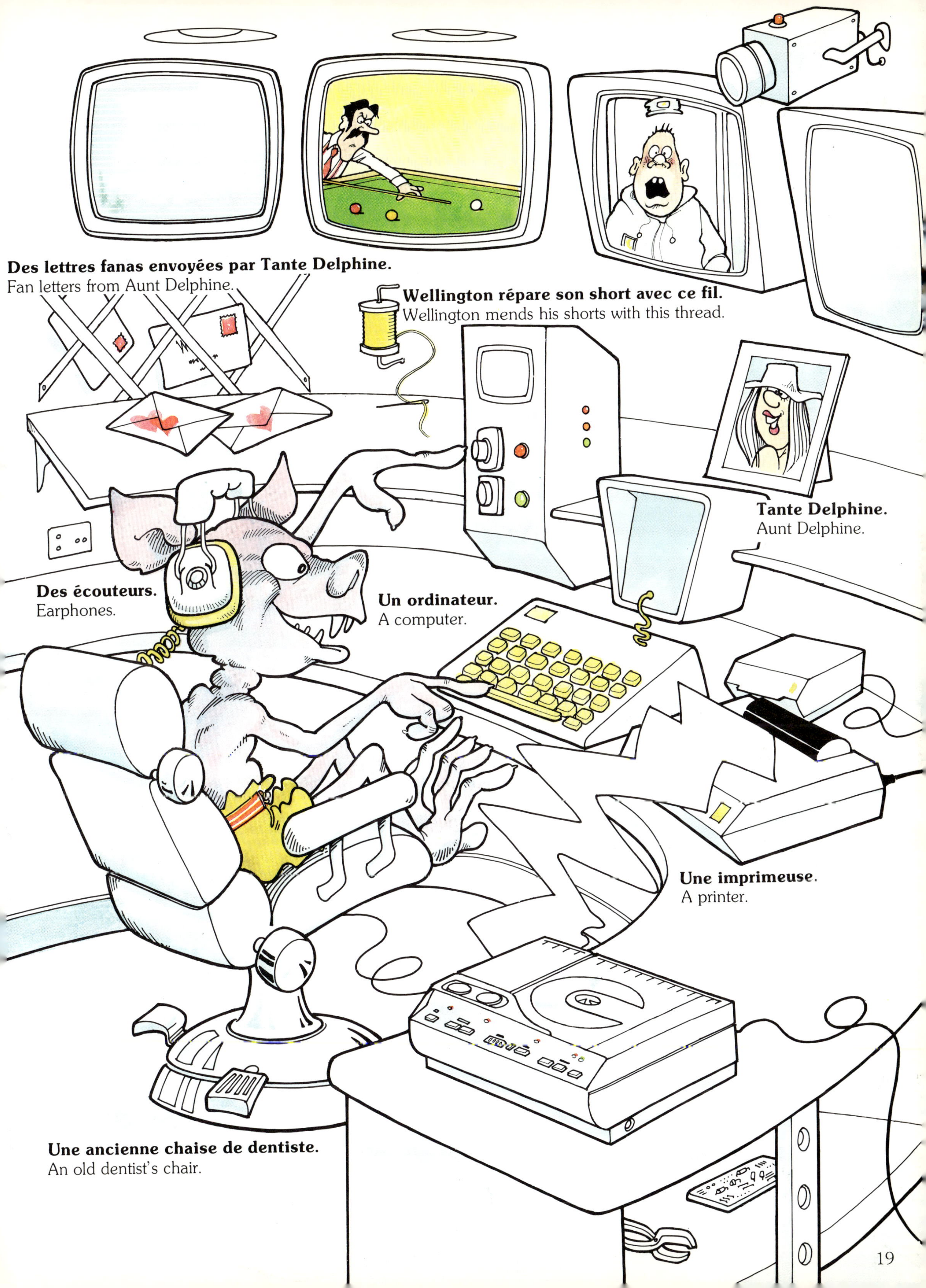
Des lettres fanas envoyées par Tante Delphine.
Fan letters from Aunt Delphine.
Wellington répare son short avec ce fil.
Wellington mends his shorts with this thread.
Tante Delphine.
Aunt Delphine.
Des écouteurs.
Earphones.
Un ordinateur.
A computer.
Une imprimeuse.
A printer.
Une ancienne chaise de dentiste.
An old dentist's chair.

Je voudrais être . . .
I'd like to be . . .

Henri Duval: Je voudrais être gardien de but professionnel.
Henry Valley: I'd like to be a professional goal-keeper.

Je voudrais jouer pour la Coupe du Monde.
I'd like to play in the World Cup.

Guy Délicieux: La vie d'un détective est formidable.
Guy Delicious: A detective's life is terrific.

Je vais arrêter le criminel le plus rusé du monde.
I'm going to arrest the cleverest criminal in the world.

Qui est le plus rusé, le criminel ou Guy?
Who's the cleverer, the criminal or Guy?

NE BOUGE PAS!
DON'T MOVE!

Anne: J'aime beaucoup les animaux.
Anne: I love animals.

Je voudrais être vétérinaire.
I'd like to be a vet.

Mais j'ai peur des piqûres.
But I'm afraid of injections.

CLIC!
CLICK!

Mimi: Je voudrais être mannequin.
Mimi: I'd like to be a model.

Oncle Albert: Je voudrais être astronaute.
Uncle Albert: I'd like to be an astronaut.

Est-ce que Salomon aime être chatonaute?
Does Solomon like being a catonaut?

Jean: Je voudrais être routier.
John: I'd like to be a truck-driver.

Est-ce que Jean conduit bien?
Is John driving well?

Welliquiz

Et toi, qu'est-ce que tu voudrais être?
And what would *you* like to be?

Speaker/speakerine?
A newscaster?

Explorateur/exploratrice?
An explorer?

Pilote d'avion?
An aeroplane pilot?

Danseur/danseuse?
A dancer?

Fermier/fermière?
A farmer?

Chauffeur/chauffeuse de taxi?
A taxi-driver?

Sapeur-pompier?
A fireman/firewomen?

Avocat?
A lawyer?

Isabelle: Je voudrais changer mon nom.
Isobel: I'd like to change my name.

Ensuite je voudrais être une chanteuse pop célèbre.
Then I'd like to be a famous pop star.

Quel est le nouveau nom d'Isabelle?
What is Isobel's new name?

Qu'est-ce que Wellington veut manger?
What does Wellington want to eat?

Combien?
How many?

Regarde ces douze dessins, puis réponds aux questions du Welliquiz.
Look at these twelve drawings, then answer the questions in the Welliquiz.

Un: Un garçon.
One: A boy.

Deux: Ces deux garçons sont des jumeaux.
Two: These two boys are twins.

Trois: Le trépied de ce télescope
Three: The tripod of this telescope

a trois pieds.
has got three legs.

Quatre: Cet avion à réaction a quatre moteurs.
Four: This jet plane has got four engines.

Cinq: Voici cinq doigts.
Five: Here are five fingers.

Six: Voici six œufs.
Six: Here are six eggs.

13 **Treize** Thirteen	**14** **Quatorze** Fourteen	**15** **Quinze** Fifteen	**16** **Seize** Sixteen	**17** **Dix-sept** Seventeen	**18** **Dix-huit** Eighteen
19 **Dix-neuf** Nineteen	**20** **Vingt** Twenty	**30** **Trente** Thirty	**40** **Quarante** Forty	**50** **Cinquante** Fifty	**60** **Soixante** Sixty
70 **Soixante-dix** Seventy	**80** **Quatre-vingts** Eighty	**90** **Quatre-vingt-dix** Ninety	**100** **Cent** A hundred	**1,000** **Mille** A thousand	

Sept: Trois et quatre font sept.
Seven: Three and four make seven.

Huit: Les araignées ont huit pattes.
Eight: Spiders have eight legs.

Neuf: Un gâteau d'anniversaire pour une personne de neuf ans.
Nine: A birthday cake for a nine-year-old.

Dix: Dix chaînes de télévision.
Ten: Ten television channels.

Onze: Une équipe de football.
Eleven: A soccer team.

Douze: Voici douze boîtes de jus d'orange.
Twelve: Here are twelve cartons of orange juice.

Welliquiz

Combien de maillots de foot rouges vois-tu?
How many red football jerseys can you see?

Les jumeaux ont neuf ans.
The twins are nine.

Combien de bougies y aura-t-il sur leur prochain gâteau d'anniversaire?
How many candles will there be on their next birthday cake?

Lequel a le plus de pieds, le trépied ou l'araignée?
Which has more legs, the tripod or the spider?

Dans le grand magasin
In the department store

Il y a beaucoup de monde dans le grand magasin.
There are a lot of people in the department store.

Mme Duval choisit un nouveau chapeau.
Mrs Valley is choosing a new hat.

Marie veut acheter une lampe.
Mary wants to buy a lamp.

Alice veut acheter un jean.
Alice wants to buy some jeans.

Pierre est fatigué.
Peter is tired.

Wellington est malade.
Wellington is ill.

Salomon est très malheureux.
Solomon is very unhappy.

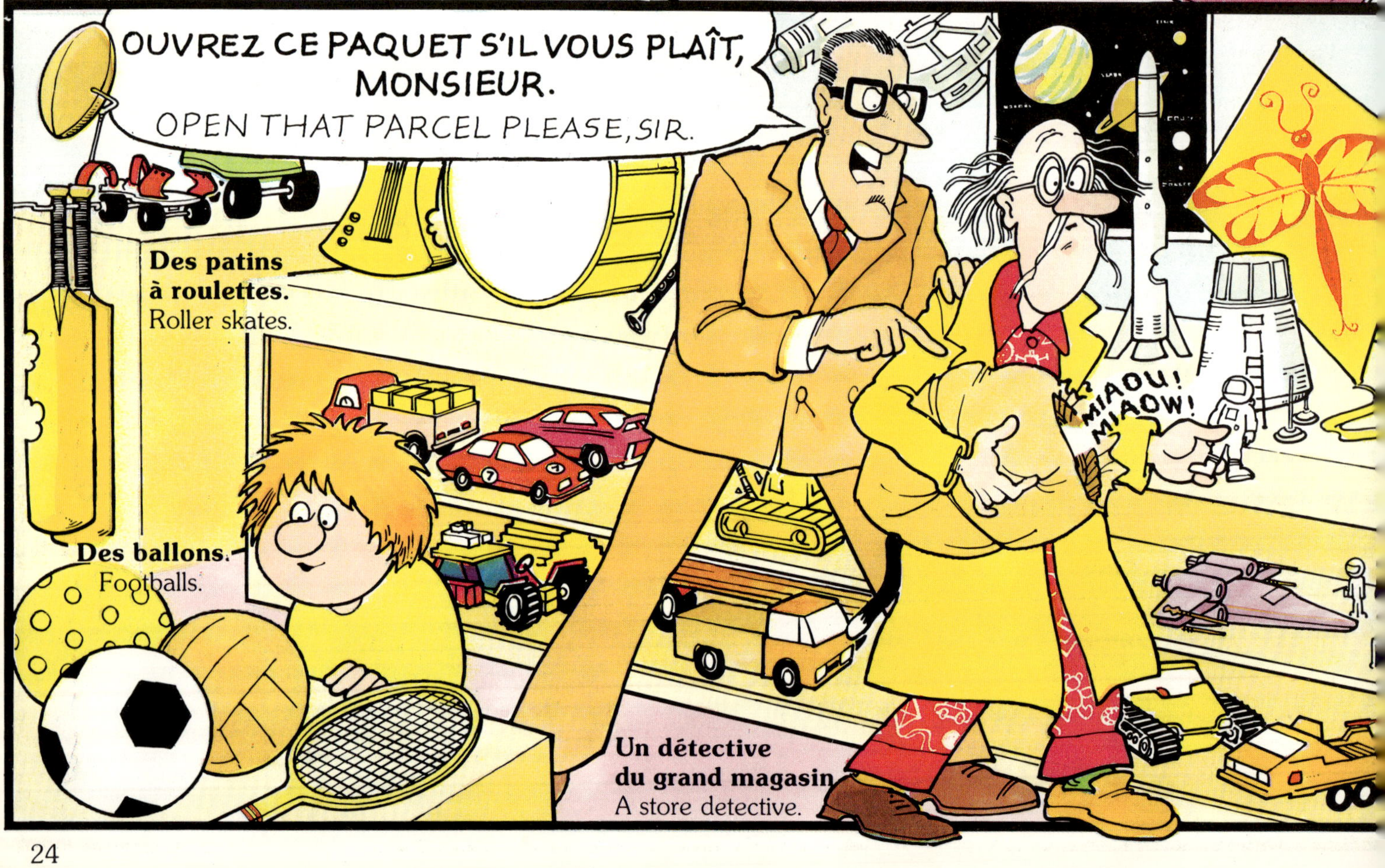

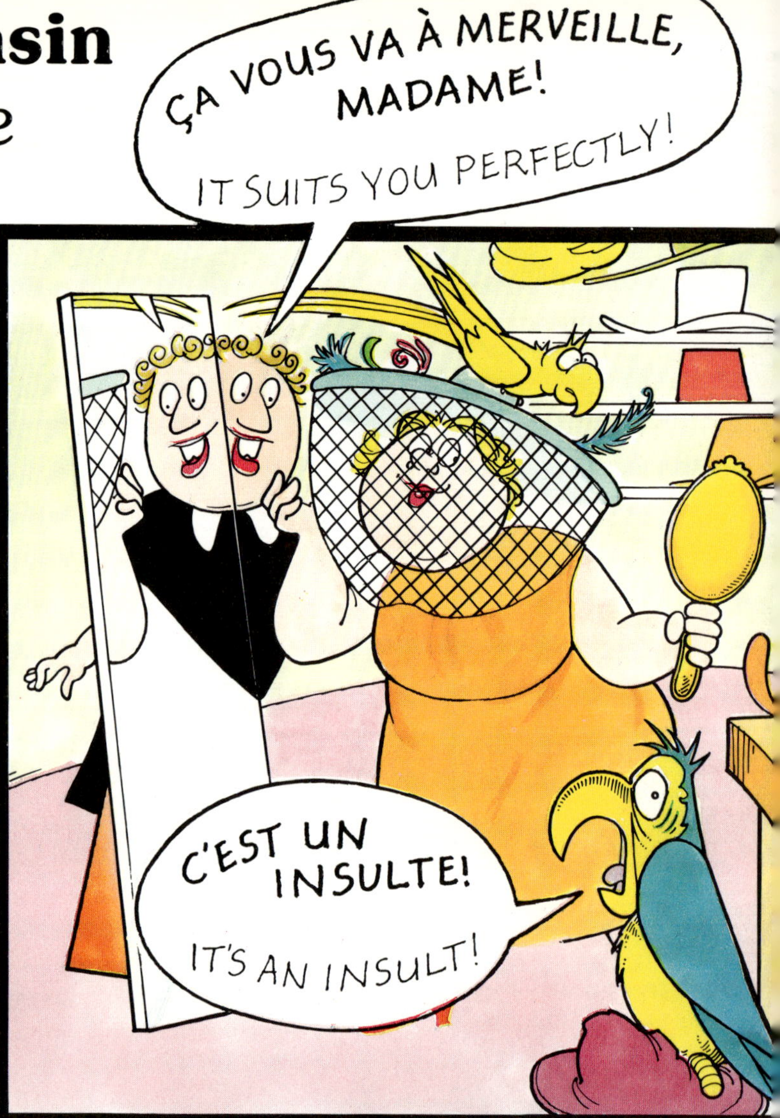

OUVREZ CE PAQUET S'IL VOUS PLAÎT, MONSIEUR.
OPEN THAT PARCEL PLEASE, SIR.

MIAOU! MIAOW!

Des patins à roulettes.
Roller skates.

Des ballons.
Footballs.

Un détective du grand magasin.
A store detective.

Est-ce que ces chaussures sont à Pierre?
Do these shoes belong to Peter?

Un robot.
A robot.

Un masque de gorille.
A gorilla mask.

Des faux nez.
False noses.

Un cowboy.
A cowboy.

Un jeu d'échecs.
A chess set.

Des lèvres en plastique.
Plastic lips.

Des cassettes.
Cassettes.

Es-tu fort en informatique?
Are you good at computers?

Choisis la réponse (page 27) qui convient aux instructions (page 26).
Choose the answer (page 27) which fits the instructions (page 26).

ENTREZ DATE DE NAISSANCE
ENTER DATE OF BIRTH

JOUR
DAY

MOIS
MONTH

ANNÉE
YEAR

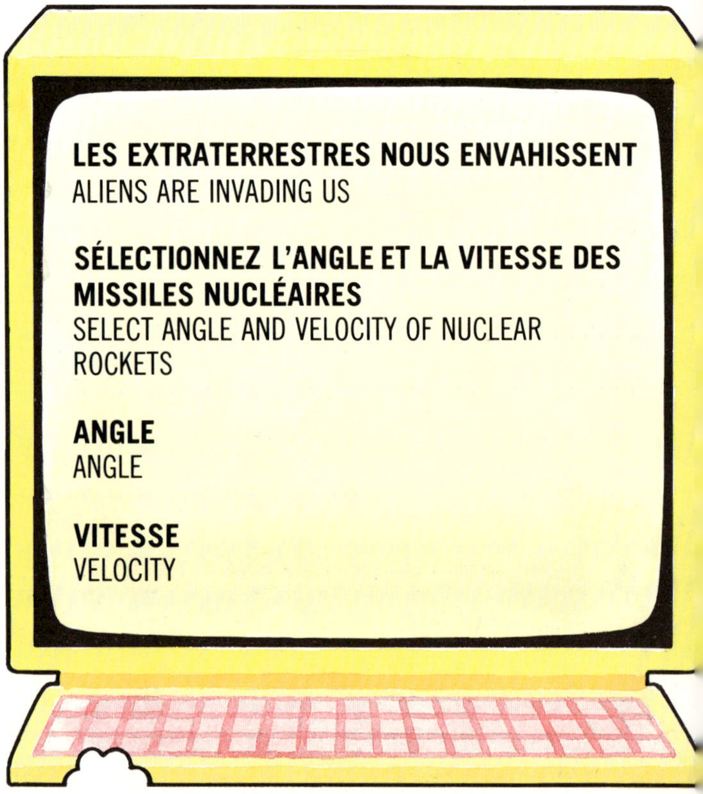

LES EXTRATERRESTRES NOUS ENVAHISSENT
ALIENS ARE INVADING US

SÉLECTIONNEZ L'ANGLE ET LA VITESSE DES MISSILES NUCLÉAIRES
SELECT ANGLE AND VELOCITY OF NUCLEAR ROCKETS

ANGLE
ANGLE

VITESSE
VELOCITY

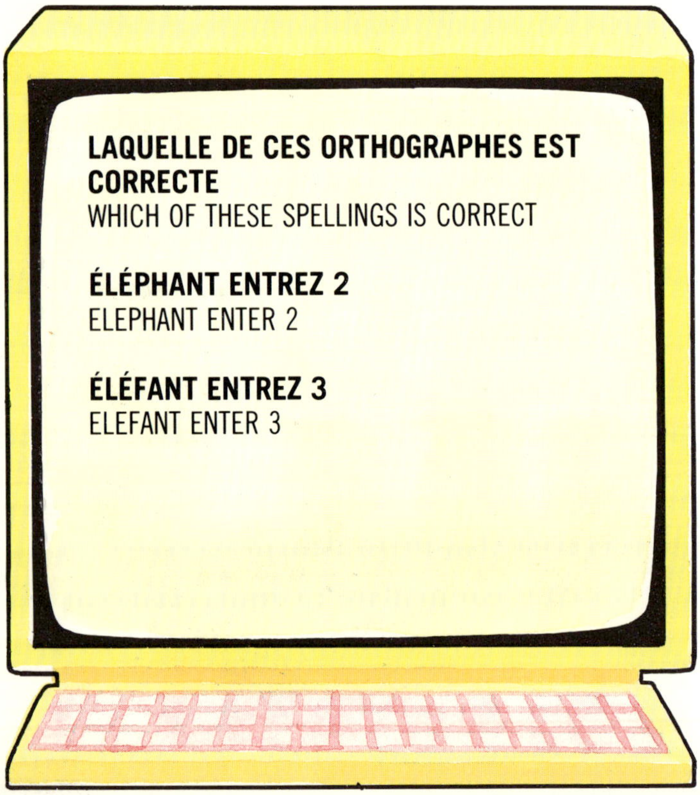

LAQUELLE DE CES ORTHOGRAPHES EST CORRECTE
WHICH OF THESE SPELLINGS IS CORRECT

ÉLÉPHANT ENTREZ 2
ELEPHANT ENTER 2

ÉLÉFANT ENTREZ 3
ELEFANT ENTER 3

VOUS ÊTES DANS LES OUBLIETTES
YOU ARE IN THE DUNGEON

IL Y A UNE CLÉ SUR LA PORTE
THERE IS A KEY IN THE DOOR

ET UNE BOÎTE SUR LE SOL
AND A BOX ON THE GROUND

POUR TOURNER LA CLÉ ENTREZ 1
TO TURN KEY ENTER 1

POUR OUVRIR LA BOÎTE ENTREZ 2
TO OPEN BOX ENTER 2

VOUS AVEZ CHOISI 2
YOU CHOSE 2

LA BOÎTE CONTENAIT UN SERPENT VÉNIMEUX
THE BOX CONTAINED A VENOMOUS SNAKE

VOUS ÊTES MORT
YOU ARE DEAD

POUR REJOUER ENTREZ Y
TO PLAY AGAIN ENTER Y

POUR ARRÊTER ENTREZ N
TO EXIT ENTER N

ERREUR
WRONG

VOUS AVEZ CHOISI 3
YOU CHOSE 3

LA BONNE RÉPONSE EST 2
THE RIGHT ANSWER IS 2

24 JUILLET 1975
24 JULY 1975

VOUS ÊTES DE FORTE VOLONTÉ ET DIGNE DE CONFIANCE
YOU ARE STRONG-WILLED AND RELIABLE

LES GENS VOUS AIMENT BIEN
PEOPLE LIKE YOU

MAIS VOUS ÊTES PARESSEUX
BUT YOU ARE LAZY

45
45

19,200 KILOMÈTRES À L'HEURE
12,000 MILES PER HOUR

FÉLICITATIONS
CONGRATULATIONS

VOUS AVEZ DÉTRUIT 90% DES EXTRATERRESTRES
YOU HAVE DESTROYED 90% OF THE ALIENS

LA TERRE EST SAUVÉE
THE EARTH IS SAVED

SI TU ES UN/UNE DE MES FANS ENTRE W
IF YOU ARE A FAN OF MINE ENTER W

SI TU ES UN GRAND/UNE GRANDE FAN ENTRE W
IF YOU ARE A GREAT FAN ENTER W

CHOISIS
CHOOSE

Wellington part en vacances
Wellington goes on holiday

C'est le début des vacances pour Wellington.
It's the beginning of the holidays for Wellington.

Il va prendre l'avion.
He's going to catch a plane.

Mais d'abord il doit se rendre à l'aéroport.
But first he's got to get to the aiport.

La voiture refuse de démarrer.
The car won't start.

Le vélo de Wellington a un pneu crevé.
Wellington's bike has got a flat tyre.

Le train est déjà parti.
The train has already left.

Il n'y a pas d'autobus.
There aren't any buses.

Heureusement, un chauffeur de camion le prend en stop.
Luckily a lorry-driver gives him a lift.

Wellington court vers l'avion.
Wellington runs to the plane.

L'hôtesse de l'air est très malheureuse.
The air hostess is very unhappy.

Qui a pris tout son argent?
Who took all her money?

C'est un désastre.
It's a disaster.

Mais Wellington n'a pas de pitié pour elle.
But Wellington does not feel sorry for her.

Il est très relaxe, très content.
He is very relaxed, very happy.

Enfin il part en vacances!
At last he's going on holiday!

Les vêtements
Clothes

Henri Duval: Le plus souvent, je porte mon short de foot,
Henry Valley: Mostly, I wear my football shorts,
une chemise, des gants, des chaussettes et des bottes.
a shirt, gloves, socks and boots.
J'ai aussi un costume.
I've also got a suit.
Mais c'est très démodé.
But it's very old-fashioned.
Mémé: Je tricote mes propres vêtements.
Granny: I knit my own clothes.
Je porte des jupes et des tricots en laine.
I wear skirts and jumpers made of wool.
Jeanne Lebon: J'aime les couleurs claires.
Jean Good: I like pale colours.
Je porte souvent un jean.
I often wear jeans.
MOI J'AIME LES COULEURS VIVES.
I LIKE BRIGHT COLOURS.

Un accident au supermarché
An accident in the supermarket

Pierre a eu un accident.
Peter has had an accident.

Les objets de son chariot sont par terre.
The things from his trolley are on the floor.

La responsable du supermarché dit qu'il doit les payer.
The manageress of the supermarket says he must pay for them.

Il y a beaucoup d'objets!
There are a lot of things!

Que sont-ils?
What are they?

Trouve les noms sur la liste de commisions de Pierre.
Find the names on Peter's shopping list.

La liste de commisions de Pierre

Peter's shopping list

1 Un kilo de farine
A kilo of flour

2 Un paquet de sucre
A packet of sugar

3 Six œufs
Six eggs

4 Un paquet de biscuits
A packet of biscuits

5 Quatre grosses tomates
Four big tomatoes

6 Un pain
A loaf of bread

7 Un poulet
A chicken

8 De la lessive
Washing powder

9 Deux brosses à dents
Two toothbrushes

10 Du savon
Soap

11 Une bouteille de shampooing
A bottle of shampoo

12 Des pommes de terre
Potatoes

13 De l'eau minérale
Mineral water

14 De l'huile pour le bain
Bath oil

15 Du sel
Salt

16 De la mousse à raser
Shaving foam

17 De la sauce
Sauce

18 Une casserole
A saucepan

19 Du poivre
Pepper

20 Cinq oranges
Five oranges

21 Du lait
Milk

22 Du beurre
Butter

J'aime manger
I like eating

Henri Duval et Mémé aiment les frites et les desserts.
Henry Valley and Granny like chips and sweets.

Yasmine prépare un pique-nique pour ses copains.
Yasmin is preparing a picnic for her friends.

Oncle Albert et Salomon adorent les sandwiches.
Uncle Albert and Solomon love sandwiches.

Soleil déteste les sandwiches.
Sunshine hates sandwiches.

Henri Duval: Mon plat préféré,
Henry Valley: My favourite dish

c'est la glace au chocolat.
is chocolate ice-cream.

Welliquiz

Combien de noms de fruits y a-t-il sur ces pages?
How many names of fruits are there on these pages?

Et combien de noms de légumes?
And how many names of vegetables?

Des sandwiches au concombre
Cucumber sandwiches

Des sandwiches au jambon et au fromage
Ham and cheese sandwiches

Un sandwich au beurre de cacahuètes et à la confiture
A peanut butter and jelly sandwich

De la laitue et des tomates.
Lettuce and tomatoes.

Des sardines.
Sardines.

Soleil: Toujours des sandwiches. Pouah!
Sunshine: Always sandwiches. Ugh!

Yasmine: Ils sont un peu bizarres, mes pains!
Yasmin: My loaves are a bit funny!

Des noix.
Nuts.

Du miel.
Honey.

Des oranges.
Oranges.

Des œufs de ferme.
Free-range eggs.

Des pommes.
Apples.

Des poires sans produits chimiques.
Unsprayed pears.

Des carottes et du céléri, élevés par Yasmine.
Carrots and celery, grown by Yasmin.

L'atelier d'Oncle Albert
Uncle Albert's workshop

Oncle Albert est dans son atelier.
Uncle Albert is in his workshop.

Il porte son pyjama, car c'est un vêtement très confortable.
He is wearing his pyjamas, as they're a very comfortable piece of clothing.

Trouve sur le pyjama: des étoiles,
Find on the pyjamas: stars,

des lunes, des vaisseaux spatiaux,
moons, space ships,

des lapins et des astronautes.
rabbits and astronauts.

Trouve aussi Wellington.
Find Wellington too.

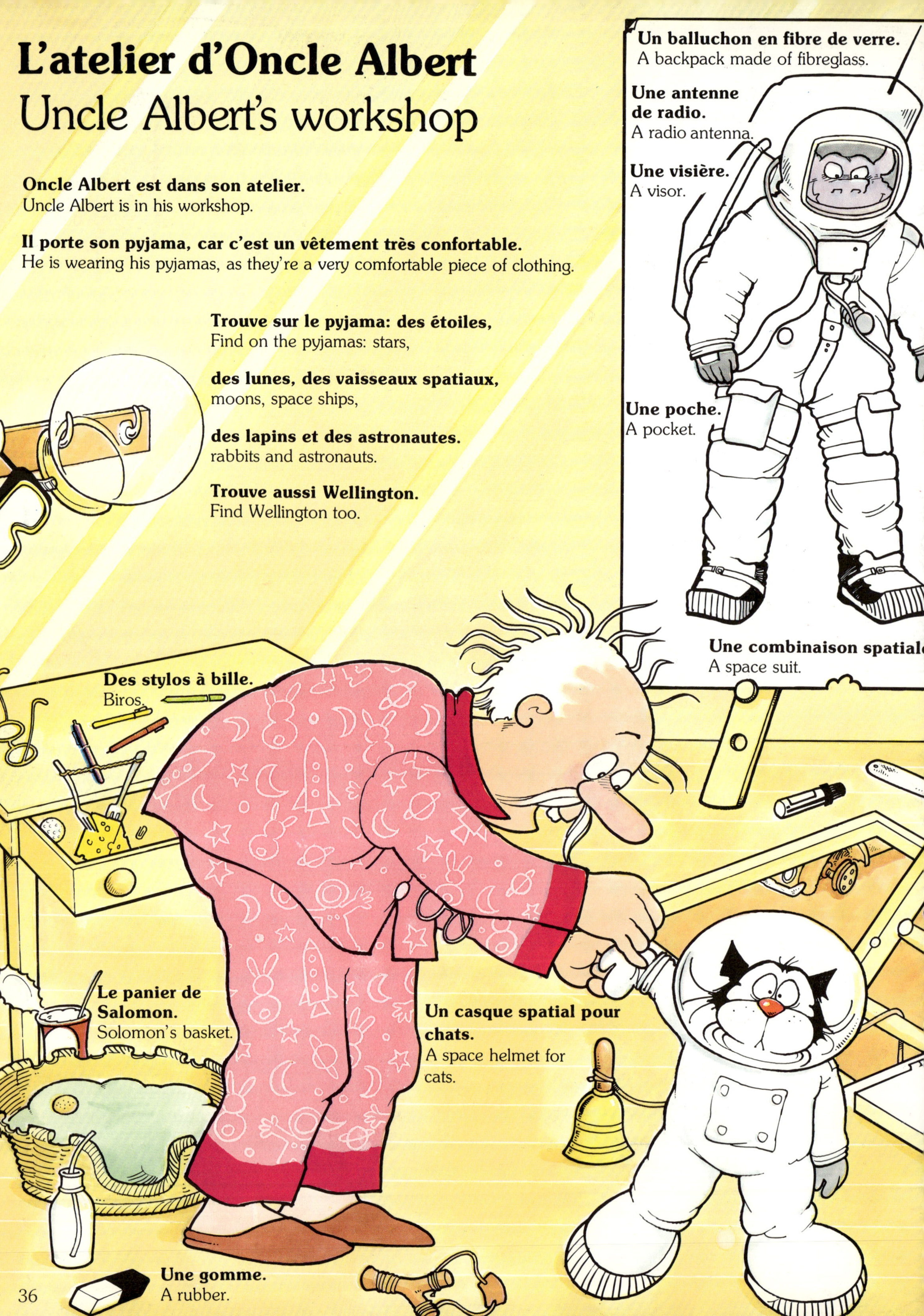

Tous les samedi soirs, Albert
Every Saturday evening Albert

et son lapin Soleil vont dans un club . . .
and his rabbit Sunshine go to a club . . .

. . . car Oncle Albert est magicien.
. . . because Uncle Albert is a magician.

Henri est à l'hôpital
Henry is in hospital

Henri a la jambe cassée.
Henry has got a broken leg.

Il se l'est cassée pendant un match de football.
He broke it during a football match.

L'équipe de football d'Henri.
Henry's football team.

Un médecin.
A doctor.

Il dit: "Je regrette, mais vous
He's saying: "I'm sorry, but you

ne pouvez pas tous entrer.
can't all come in.

Vous êtes trop nombreux."
There are too many of you."

Un manteau blanc.
A white coat.

Une montre.
A watch.

Une infirmière.
A nurse.

Une table roulante.
A trolley.

Des médicaments et un thermomètre.
Medicines and a thermometer.

Tante Delphine a fait un gâteau au chocolat pour Henri.
Aunt Delphine made a chocolate cake for Henry.

Elle n'est pas une très bonne cuisinière.
She isn't a very good cook.

Une robe de chambre.
A dressing gown.

Un oreiller.
A pillow.

Une couverture.
A blanket.

Une table de nuit.
A bedside table.

Un jeu électronique.
A computer game.

Des pantoufles.
Slippers.

Le cadeau d'Anne pour Henri.
Anne's present to Henry.

Comment ça s'appelle en français?
What is its name in French?

Vivent les champions!
Long live the champions!

LE COUPLE NUMÉRO 12 EST FORMIDABLE!
COUPLE NUMBER 12 ARE FANTASTIC!

QUEL COSTUME MAGNIFIQUE!
WHAT A MAGNIFICENT COSTUME!

Il y a un concours de patinage à la patinoire.
There is a skating competition at the ice-rink.

Le présentateur va annoncer les finalistes.
The announcer is going to announce the finalists.

2

...MIMI ET AHMED (NUMÉRO QUATRE
...MIMI AND AHMED (NUMBER FOUR)

ET PAMÉLA ET FRÉDÉRIQUE (QUINZE)
AND PAMELA AND FREDERICK (FIFTEEN).

ÉPATANT!
FANTASTIC!

NOUS ALLONS GAGNER À TOUT PRIX.
WE ARE GOING TO WIN AT ANY PRICE.

3

QUELLE MAUVAISE ACTION!
WHAT AN EVIL DEED!

JE VENGERAI MIMI!
I WILL AVENGE MIMI!

AÏE! QUELLE HORREUR!
AAAAH! HOW TERRIBLE!
QUEL DÉSASTRE!
WHAT A DISASTER!
Tout à coup Mimi tombe.
Suddenly Mimi falls.

SCROUNCH!
CRUNCH!
La vengeance de Wellington . . .
Wellington's vengeance . . .

QUELQU'UN A MIS DU CHEWING-GUM SUR MON PATIN!
SOMEBODY PUT CHEWING-GUM ON MY SKATE!
REGARDEZ! C'EST UN PAQUET DE CHEWING-GUM!
LOOK! IT'S A PACKET OF CHEWING-GUM!
QU'EST-CE QUI SE PASSE?
WHAT'S GOING ON?

VOICI LES GAGNANTS: MIMI ET AHMED.
HERE ARE THE WINNERS: MIMI AND AHMED.
VIVENT LES CHAMPIONS!
LONG LIVE THE CHAMPIONS!
ILS SONT DÉLICIEUX, CES PATINS!
THESE SKATES ARE DELICIOUS!

Les animaux favoris
Pets

Voici dix propriétaires avec leurs animaux favoris.
Here are ten owners with their pets.

Quand tu vois ★★, choisis le mot correct dans cette liste.
When you see ★★, choose the right word from this list.

poissons rouges goldfish	**hamster** hamster	**chien** dog	**canard** duck	**chat** cat
souris blanches white mice	**Mme Duval** Mrs Valley	**cheval** horse	**serpent** snake	**lapin** rabbit

Henri Duval: J'ai beaucoup d'animaux.
Henry Valley: I've got lots of pets.

Elles sont géniales, mes ★★.
My ★★ are great.

Plume: ★★ croit qu'elle est ma propriétaire.
Feather: ★★ thinks that she's my owner.

C'est pas vrai! C'est moi son propriétaire!
It's not true! I'm *her* owner!

Guy Délicieux: Mon animal s'appelle Idiot.
Guy Delicious: My pet is called Idiot.

C'est un ★★ très intelligent.
He's a very clever ★★.

Anne: Mon animal préféré, c'est mon Pégase.
Anne: My favourite animal is my Pegasus.

C'est un ★★.
He's a ★★.

Alice: Cet animal est à ma sœur.
Alice: This animal belongs to my sister.

Mais il m'adore aussi.
But he loves me too.

Il s'appelle Minus et c'est un ★★.
He's called Minus and he's a ★★.

Welliquiz

Qu'est-ce que Wellington a mangé?
What has Wellington eaten?

(Regarde le bébé, Henri, et Oncle Georges.)
(Look at the baby, Henry and Uncle George.)

Quel sport?
Which sport?

Voici six personnes.
Here are six people.

Chacun essaie de pratiquer un sport.
Each one is trying to do a sport.

Mais ils n'ont pas tous les accessoires corrects.
But they haven't got all the right equipment.

Trouve les personnes qui doivent faire un échange d'accessoires.
Find the people who should exchange equipment.

David est lanceur de disques.
David is a discus thrower.

Il doit faire un échange avec ★★.
He should exchange with ★★.

Oncle Albert adore le baseball.
Uncle Albert loves baseball.

Il doit faire un échange avec ★★.
He should exchange with ★★.

Mémé est forte en patins à roulettes.
Granny is good at roller skating.

Elle doit faire un échange avec ★★.
She should exchange with ★★.

Laure aime jouer au tennis.
Laura likes playing tennis.

Elle doit faire un échange avec ★★.
She should exchange with ★★.

Mimi est championne de patinage sur glace.
Mimi is a champion ice-skater.

Elle doit faire un échange avec ★★.
She should exchange with ★★.

En été, Henri joue souvent au cricket.
In summer, Henry often plays cricket.

Il doit faire un échange avec ★★.
He should exchange with ★★.

Est-ce qu'ils disent la vérité?

Are they telling the truth?

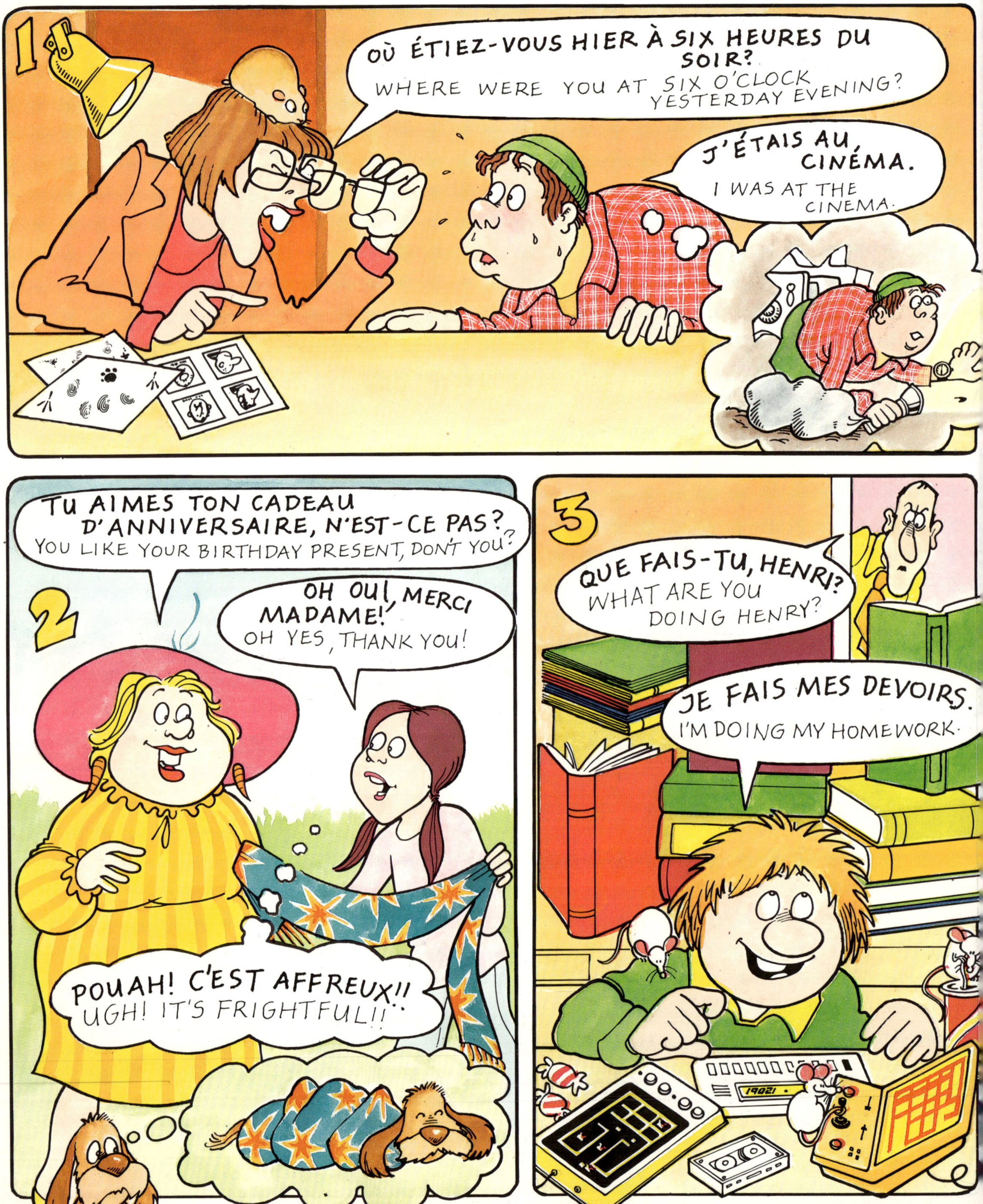

2

TU AIMES TON CADEAU D'ANNIVERSAIRE, N'EST-CE PAS?
YOU LIKE YOUR BIRTHDAY PRESENT, DON'T YOU?

OH OUI, MERCI MADAME!
OH YES, THANK YOU!

POUAH! C'EST AFFREUX!!
UGH! IT'S FRIGHTFUL!!

3

QUE FAIS-TU, HENRI?
WHAT ARE YOU DOING HENRY?

JE FAIS MES DEVOIRS.
I'M DOING MY HOMEWORK.

Es-tu un bon détective?
Are you a good detective?

Est-ce que le criminel dit la vérité?
Is the criminal telling the truth?

Est-ce que Jeanne dit la vérité?
Is Jean telling the truth?

Et Henri?
And Henry?

Et M. Lebon?
And Mr Good?

Et Wellington?
And Wellington?

La maison des bizarreries
The house of oddities

Quand tu vois ★★, trouve la fin correcte de la phrase. Toutes les fins sont dans la liste.
When you see ★★ find the correct ending of the sentence. All the endings are in the list.

Luc a les cheveux noirs, mais ★★
Luke has got black hair, but ★★

Il y a du papier peint sur les murs et ★★
There is wallpaper on the walls and ★★

Le téléviseur est allumé, mais ★★
The television is on, but ★★

La laine de Mémé est bleue, mais ★★
Granny's wool is blue, but ★★

Le chat court vite, ★★
The cat is running fast, ★★

Le bain moussant est jaune, mais ★★
The bubble bath is yellow, but ★★

RENDS-MOI MON BONNET, PAPA!
GIVE ME BACK MY HAT, DADDY!

Le bébé est très jeune, mais ★★
The baby is very young, but ★★

Liste
List

il n'est pas branché!
it's not plugged in!

parce qu'il a peur de la souris!
because it's afraid of the mouse!

le pull qu'elle tricote est rouge!
the jersey which she's knitting is red!

l'eau est verte!
the water is green!

les cheveux qui tombent sont blonds!
the hair which is falling is blonde!

sur le plancher aussi!
on the floor too!

il parle comme un adulte!
he talks like an adult!

Welliquiz

Trouve d'autres bizarreries.
Find some more oddities.

(Regarde les posters,
(Look at the posters,

le chien,
the dog,

la chaise,
the chair,

la glace,
the mirror,

et Tante Delphine.)
and Aunt Delphine.)

Qu'est-ce qu'il mange, Wellington?
What is Wellington eating?

Et qu'est-ce qu'il a mordu?
And what has he bitten?

Mes objets préférés
My favourite things

Voici douze personnes, et leurs objets préférés.
Here are twelve people, and their favourite things.

Trouve les objets préférés de chaque personne.
Find each person's favourite things.

Par exemple: Mme Duval aime les grands chapeaux à fleurs.
For example: Mrs Valley likes big hats with flowers.

Anne
Anne

Laure
Laura

Le foot, les frites et les souris blanches.
Football, chips and white mice.

Ahmed
Ahmed

Mme Duval
Mrs Valley

Les grands chapeaux à fleurs.
Big hats with flowers.

Le maquillage et les patins à roulettes.
Make-up and roller skates.

Les lapins et la magie.
Rabbits and magic.

Son chien et les couleurs claires.
Her dog and pale colours.

Le billard et les serpents.
Snooker and snakes.

Oncle Albert
Uncle Albert

Henri Duval
Henry Valley

Jeanne
Jean

Isabelle
Isobel

Oncle Georges
Uncle George

Lune
Moon

Pierre
Peter

Wellington
Wellington

Le foot et les vêtements à froufrous.
Football and frilly clothes.

Les objets qui sont bons à manger.
Objects which are good to eat.

Les films et les livres policiers.
Detective films and books.

Marie et les sandwiches.
Mary and sandwiches.

Mimi et le patinage.
Mimi and skating.

Les animaux.
Animals.

J'ai rêvé . . .
I dreamed . . .

Voici cinq rêves.
Here are five dreams.

Yasmine: J'ai rêvé de Superman.
Yasmin: I dreamed about Superman.

Henri Duval: J'ai rêvé de glaces et de frites.
Henry Valley: I dreamed about ice-creams and chips.

Quel rêve merveilleux!
What a wonderful dream!

Isabelle: J'étais en Australie.
Isobel: I was in Australia.

J'étais un mouton, et mes amis aussi!
I was a sheep, and my friends too!

Oncle Albert: J'ai rêvé que je volais.
Uncle Albert: I dreamed that I was flying.

Un géant me donnait une paire d'ailes.
A giant gave me a pair of wings.

Welliquiz

Wellington a rêvé d'un champion. Qui est-ce?
Wellington dreamed about a champion. Who is it?

Regarde les moutons. Qui sont-ils?
Look at the sheep. Who are they?

Est ce que Salomon aime voler?
Does Solomon like flying?

La course de lits
The bed race

Henri est furieux.
Henry is furious.

Il veut jouer au football.
He wants to play football.

C'est un match très important.
It's a very important match.

Henri est la vedette de son équipe.
Henry is the star of his team.

BRAVO, HENRI!
WELL DONE, HENRY!

IL EST GÉNIAL!
HE'S FANTASTIC!

Mais hélas! Il ne peut pas jouer.
But alas! He cannot play.

Heureusement, Laure a une idée...
Luckily, Laura has an idea...

ÉCOUTE
LISTEN

... une course de lits contre l'équipe Duval!
... a bed race against the Valley team.

Voici l'équipe Laure.
Here is the Laura team.

L'équipe Laure va vite.
The Laura team goes fast.

L'équipe Duval est rapide aussi.
The Valley team is fast too.

Mais tout à coup . . .
But suddenly . . .

Catastrophe! L'équipe Duval s'arrête.
Catastrophe! The Valley team stops.

Henri dégage le ballon.
Henry clears the ball.

Victoire à l'équipe Laure!
Victory for the Laura team!

Henri est la vedette de son équipe!
Henry is the star of his team!

Welliquiz super-final
Super-final Welliquiz

Wellilesson 2

It's a long time since you had a lesson from me. Concentrate.

English humans say ***the boy*** and ***the girl*** (they're not very good at conversation). But French humans say **le garçon** and **la fille** – well, it's a different language. **Garçon** is a masculine noun, as you might expect, and **fille** is feminine. All nouns in French are either masculine or feminine. **Un couteau** – ***a knife*** – is masculine, but **une fourchette** – ***a fork*** – is feminine. How did they work out a system like that! Nouns have **le** or **la**, meaning ***the***, in front of them; or else **un** or **une**, meaning ***a/an.*** **Un garçon** is ***a boy***, in case you didn't know, and **une fille** is ***a girl.***

If a noun is masculine, the adjective which describes it must be masculine too. That is a Wellirule which has to be OBEYED. If a noun is feminine, the adjective describing it has to be in the feminine form. This usually means adding an ***e*** to the adjective. For example **un garçon français** is ***a French boy*** (if you don't know that by now, give up) and **une fille française** is ***a French girl.*** Are you getting the idea?

In my final (sob) quiz, you sometimes have to choose between a masculine form and a feminine form. Decisions, decisions. For example, **Es-tu français/française?** (well, are you or aren't you?). Because of tradition, the masculine form is given first. That's a human system, of course. Creatures like me don't have silly rules like that (actually, I don't follow any rules at all).

That's enough of this lesson. I hope you've learned something, though I doubt it. But you'll never be able to tell me you still don't understand about masculine-and-feminine-and-nouns-and-adjectives-and-le-and-la-and knives-and-forks-etcetera-etcetera because I can make myself invisible to you because I'm the greatest cleverest super-fantastic

WELLINGTON!

Choisis les bonnes réponses!
Choose the right answers!

1 Es-tu français/française?
Are you French?
Non, je suis
No, I'm
A anglais/anglaise
English
B irlandais/irlandaise
Irish
C écossais/écossaise
Scottish
D gallois/galloise
Welsh
E britannique
British
F allemand/allemande
German
G italien/italienne
Italian
H espagnol/espagnole
Spanish

2 Étudies-tu le français à l'école?
Do you do French at school?
A Oui, c'est ma matière préférée.
Yes, it's my favourite subject.
B Non, pas encore.
No, not yet.
C Oui, mais c'est difficile.
Yes, but it's difficult.

3 Parles-tu bien le français?
Do you speak French well?
A Oui, comme un Français/une Française!
Yes, like a Frenchman/a Frenchwoman!
B Non, pas très bien.
No, not very well.
C Euh . . . non.
Er . . . no.

4 Es-tu déjà allé/allée en France?
Have you ever been to France?
A Oui, c'était formidable!
Yes, it was terrific!
B Non, mais je veux y aller.
No, but I want to go.

5 Qu'est-ce que tu aimes faire pendant tes heures libres?
What do you like doing in your spare time?
J'aime
I like

A faire des promenades à vélo.
going for bike rides.
B faire la cuisine.
cooking.
C collectionner des timbres.
collecting stamps.
D monter à cheval.
riding.
E lire.
reading.
F nager.
swimming.
G regarder la télévision.
watching television.
H jouer avec mes copains/copines.
playing with my friends.
I embrouiller les adultes.
confusing grown-ups.

6 À ton avis, est-ce que Wellington enseigne bien le français?
In your opinion, does Wellington teach French well?
A Oui, mais je préfère mon prof humain.
Yes, but I prefer my human teacher.
B Non, il est difficile à suivre.
No, he's difficult to follow.
C Oui, il est super-formidable!
Yes, he's super-terrific!

7 As-tu un correspondant français ou une correspondante française?
Have you got a French pen-friend (boy or girl)?
A Oui, nous nous écrivons souvent.
Yes, we write to each other often.
B Non, je suis trop jeune.
No, I'm too young.
C Oui, il/elle s'appelle ★★.
Yes, he/she is called ★★.

8 Laquelle de ces personnes aimerais-tu avoir comme correspondant/correspondante?
Which of these people would you like to have as a pen-friend?
A Oncle Albert.
Uncle Albert.
B Henri Duval.
Henry Valley.
C Mémé.
Granny.
D Laure.
Laura.
E Wellington.
(Si tu choisis E, il y a un problème:
(If you choose E, there is a problem:
Delphine est la seule à connaître l'adresse de Wellington.)
Delphine is the only person who knows Wellington's address.)

9 Combien de frères et sœurs as-tu?
How many brothers and sisters have you got?
A Je n'en ai pas.
I haven't got any.
B Beaucoup – trop!
A lot – too many!
C J'ai ★★ frères et ★★ sœurs.
I've got ★★ brothers and ★★ sisters.

10 Es-tu grand/grande ou petit/petite?
Are you tall or small?
Je suis
I'm
A grand/grande.
tall.
B petit/petite.
small.
moyen/moyenne.
medium-sized.

11 Comment est ton caractère?
What is your character like?
Je suis
I'm
A amusant/amusante.
funny, amusing.
B paresseux/paresseuse.
lazy.
C rêveur/rêveuse.
dreamy.
(Comme Oncle Albert.)
(Like Uncle Albert.)
D patient/patiente.
patient.
E généreux/généreuse.
generous.
F attaché/attachée aux animaux.
fond of animals.
(Comme Anne.)
(Like Anne.)
G indépendant/indépendante.
independent.
H gourmand/gourmande.
greedy
(Comme Mémé.)
(Like Granny.)
I sympathique.
nice.
J cool.
cool.

12 Comment est le caractère de Wellington?
What is Wellington's character like?
Il est
He is
A aimable.
pleasant.
B méchant.
naughty.
C intelligent.
clever.
D égoïste.
self-centred.
E populaire.
popular.
F charmant.
charming.

Wellijeux
Welligames

Wellilesson 3

You wouldn't expect a lesson on a games page, would you? Don't worry (much). This is a very short lesson, and I'm only going to say that you must play the games IN FRENCH wherever you can. Don't look at the English instructions until you've tried and tried and TRIED to understand them in French. That's all!

WELLIGAME 1

Cherche dans ce livre dix mots français:
Find in this book ten French words:

1 **Un mot qui commence par un W:**
A word which begins with a W: Wellington!
2 **Un mot qui commence par un E:**
3 **Un mot qui commence par un L:**
4 **Un mot qui commence par un L:**
5 **Un mot qui commence par un I:**
6 **Un mot qui commence par un N:**
7 **Un mot qui commence par un G:**
8 **Un mot qui commence par un T:**
9 **Un mot qui commence par un O:**
10 **Un mot qui commence par un N:**

WELLIGAME 2

Voici les débuts et les fins de dix phrases.
Here are the beginnings and the endings of ten sentences.

Assemble les bons débuts et les bonnes fins.
Put the right beginnings and endings together.

DÉBUTS
BEGINNINGS

1 **Henri Duval est fort en**
Henry Valley is good at
2 **Le perroquet**
The parrot
3 **Yasmine a rêvé**
Yasmin dreamed
4 **Mimi et Ahmed**
Mimi and Ahmed
5 **Le bébé a**
The baby has got
6 **Salomon et Soleil**
Solomon and Sunshine

FINS
ENDINGS

A **de Superman.**
about Superman.
B **un canard en plastique.**
a plastic duck.
C **foot.**
football.
D **sont à Oncle Albert.**
belong to Uncle Albert.
E **sont des champions de patinage.**
are skating champions.
F **s'appelle Plume.**
is called Feather.

WELLIGAME 3

Qu'est-ce que tu sais?
What do you know?

Teste-toi!
Test yourself!

1 **Dans quel pays y a-t-il le plus de langues?**
Which country has the most languages?
2 **Quel est le pays le plus peuplé?**
Which country has the most inhabitants?
3 **Quel est le poisson le plus rapide?**
Which fish swims the fastest?
4 **Quel âge avait le poisson rouge le plus vieux du monde?**
How old was the oldest goldfish in the world?
5 **Dans quel pays les écoliers et les écolières travaillent-ils le plus?**
In which country do schoolchildren work the hardest?
6 **Dans quel pays est-ce qu'on servait aux enfants malades des souris épluchées?**
In which country used they to give sick children skinned mice to eat?

WELLIGAME 4

Voici une liste de personnes.
Here is a list of people.

Toutes ces personnes sont dans ce livre.
All these people are in this book.

Voici aussi de petites descriptions.
Here too are some short descriptions.

Cherche la bonne description pour chaque personne.
Find the right description for each person.

1 **Oncle Albert.**
Uncle Albert.
2 **Henri Duval.**
Henry Valley.
3 **Lune.**
Moon.
4 **Ahmed.**
Ahmed.
5 **Mémé.**
Granny.

A **Elle a les cheveux noirs, et elle rit beaucoup.**
She has got black hair, and she laughs a lot.
B **Ses animaux favoris sont des champions.**
Her pets are champions.
C **Il est inventeur et magicien.**
He is an inventor and a magician.
D **Il est beau, et il est champion de patinage.**
He is good-looking, and he is a skating champion.
E **Il n'aime pas les mariages, mais il adore le football.**
He doesn't like weddings, but he loves football.

WELLIGAME 5

Quel âge a ton père? Et ton prof? Ta tante?
How old is your father? And your teacher? Your aunt?

Donne ces instructions à ton père.
Give your father these instructions.

1 **Choisis le numéro du mois de ton anniversaire (janvier = 1, février = 2, mars = 3, avril = 4, mai = 5, juin = 6, juillet = 7, août = 8, septembre = 9, octobre = 10, novembre = 11, décembre = 12).**
Choose the number of the month of your birthday (January = 1, February = 2, March = 3, April = 4, May = 5, June = 6, July = 7, August = 8, September = 9, October = 10, November = 11, December = 12).
2 **Multiplie le numéro par 2.**
Multiply the number by 2.
3 **Ajoute 5.**
Add 5.
4 **Multiplie par 50.**
Multiply by 50.
5 **Ajoute ton âge.**
Add your age.
6 **Retranche 250.**
Subtract 250.

Il y a deux résultats possibles:
There are two possible results:

1 **Le numéro final a 3 chiffres.**
The final number has 3 figures.

Le premier chiffre = le mois de l'anniversaire de ton père.
The first number = the month of your father's birthday.

Les deux autres chiffres = son âge!
The two other figures = his age!

2 **Le numéro final a 4 chiffres.**
The final number has 4 figures.

Les deux premiers chiffres = le mois.
The first two numbers = the month.

Les deux autres = l'âge!
The two others = the age!

WELLIGAME 6

Voici des listes de mots (en français).
Here are some lists of words (in French).

La dernière lettre de chaque mot est la première lettre du mot suivant.
The last letter of each word is the first letter of the next word.

Quels sont les mots?
What are the words?

1 **PYJAMASTRONAUTEXEMPLESTÉLÉVISEUROUGE (Six mots**
Six words)
2 **CLUBOUMÉDECINONEUFOOTANTE (Sept mots**
Seven words)
3 **COULEURSOURISOUVENTOUJOURSHORT (Cinq mots**
Five words)

Réponses
Answers

WELLIGAME 1: Examples: **2** Exemple. **3 & 4** Lapin, Lune. **5** Infirmière. **6 & 10** Nouveau, Non. **7** Géant. **8** Train. **9** Oncle.
WELLIGAME 2: 1C. 2F. 3A. 4E. 5B. 6D.
WELLIGAME 3: 1 India. **2** China. **3** American sailfish. **4** 36. **5** Japan. **6** Ancient Egypt.
WELLIGAME 4: 1C. 2E. 3A. 4D. 5B.
WELLIGAME 6: Pyjama, astronaute, exemple, est, téléviseur, rouge. **2** Club, boum, médecin, non, neuf, foot, tante. **3** Couleurs, souris, souvent, toujours, short.

Wellilistes
Wellilists

Wellilesson 4

This is my last (sob) lesson. You'll be glad to know that it's even shorter than Wellilesson 3. I have to leave space for all these lists of words. The lesson is: read and learn all the words!

Bonjour et au revoir
Hello and goodbye

Salut
Hi

Bonjour
Hello

Bonsoir
Good evening

Au revoir
Goodbye

À bientôt
See you soon

Des panneaux
Signs

Ouvert
Open

Fermé
Closed

Tirez
Pull

Poussez
Push

Entrée
Entrance

Sortie
Exit

Défendu/Défense
Forbidden

Privé
Private

Questions
Questions

Où?
Where?

Combien?
How much, or how many?

Quand?
When?

Pourquoi?
Why?

Comment?
How?

À quelle heure?
What time?

Ça va?
How's things?

Les Directions
Directions

À droite
On the right

À gauche
On the left

Tout droit
Straight ahead

Derrière
Behind

Devant
In front of

Près
Near

Loin
Far

Les jours de la semaine
Days of the week

undi
Monday

mardi
Tuesday

mercredi
Wednesday

eudi
Thursday

vendredi
Friday

samedi
Saturday

dimanche
Sunday

Les saisons de l'année
The seasons of the year

Au printemps
n spring

En été
n summer

En automne
In autumn

En hiver
In winter

Les parties du corps
Parts of the body

a tête
Head

e visage
ace

a bouche
Mouth

e nez
Nose

'oreille
ar

es yeux (un œil)
yes (an eye)

es sourcils
yebrows

es dents
eeth

e menton
hin

a joue
heek

es cils
yelashes

Le cou
Neck

Le bras
Arm

Le coude
Elbow

La main
Hand

Les doigts
Fingers

L'estomac
Stomach

Les hanches
Hips

La jambe
Leg

Le pied
Foot

La cheville
Ankle

Le genou
Knee

Les pays
Countries

L'Australie
Australia

L'Autriche
Austria

L'Argentine
Argentina

La Belgique
Belgium

Le Canada
Canada

Les Iles Anglo-Normandes
The Channel Islands

La Chine
China

Le Danemark
Denmark

L'Angleterre
England

La République Irlandaise
Ireland/Eire

La Finlande
Finland

La France
France

L'Allemagne
Germany

La Grèce
Greece

Les Pays-Bas
The Netherlands

La Hongrie
Hungary

L'Iran
Iran

L'Iraq
Iraq

L'Italie
Italy

La Jordanie
Jordan

Le Mexique
Mexico

Le Luxembourg
Luxembourg

Le Japon
Japan

L'Irlande du Nord
Northern Ireland

La Norvège
Norway

La Nouvelle Zélande
New Zealand

La Pologne
Poland

Le Portugal
Portugal

La Russie
Russia

L'Écosse
Scotland

L'Afrique du Sud
South Africa

L'Amérique du Sud
South America

L'Espagne
Spain

La Suède
Sweden

La Suisse
Switzerland

La Turquie
Turkey

Les États-Unis
The United States of America

Le Pays de Galles
Wales

La Yugoslavie
Yugoslavia

Pour les parents
For parents

Wellington's Way to Learn French is a method of increasing children's knowledge of French. All the French in the book has an English translation immediately underneath it, to help readers who know little or no French. But more and more French words can be brought in as the reader proceeds through the book. Words are often repeated, in new and different contexts, so he/she will gradually become familiar with them. When guiding your child's reading, encourage him/her to concentrate on the pictures first, as they tell a great deal of the story. The French words will then be easier to understand.

A child who has already learned some French will recognize many of the French words and sentences in *Wellington's Way to Learn French*. He/She may want to read the French only, covering up the English translation with a piece of paper. Encourage him/her to go even further, and name some of the many things in the pictures which are not labelled. However, do not encourage him/her to try to invent French sentences. They will almost certainly be wrong, and should not get into a learner's head.

Since one of the main aims in learning French is to speak the language, much of Wellington's text is the kind of thing that people *say*. Readers will learn some of the most basic questions and answers, for example **Comment t'appelles-tu?** – *What's your name?* and **J'ai dix ans** – *I'm ten years old.*

In order to speak French, readers must know how to pronounce it. On pages 6 and 7 Wellington gives several ways of learning pronunciation. Read these pages carefully, with your child, as it is important not to learn wrong pronunciations.

After pages 6 and 7, the best way to read the book is straight through from beginning to end. People, words and sentences will appear and reappear in the right order. It is also possible to dip into the book, and read pages out of order.

Encourage your child to answer the questions, such as those in the short *Welliquizzes* and in the big quiz on pages 56 and 57. It does not matter how simply the answers are given – there is no need to answer in long sentences. The quizzes, like the games on pages 58 and 59, are there to interest and amuse, as well as to teach.

Most important of all, encourage your child to enjoy French, as something challenging, interesting and fun. That is Wellington's way to learn French.